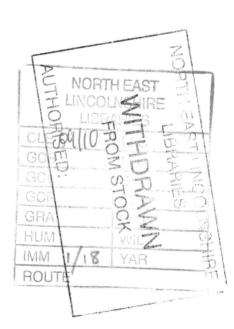

Series consultant: Dr Dorothy Rowe

The author and publisher would like to thank
the staff and pupils of the following schools for their help
in making this book: St Vincent de Paul Roman Catholic
School, Westminster; Mayfield Primary School,
Cambridge; Swavesey Village College, Cambridge.

A CIP catalogue record for this book
is available from the British Library.

ISBN-10: 0-7136-6332-4
ISBN-13: 978-07136-6332-7

Reprinted 2004, 2005, 2006
First paperback edition published 2002
First published in hardback in 1997 by
A & C Black Publishers Ltd
38 Soho Square, London W1D 3HB
www.acblack.com

Typeset in 15/19 pt Sabon Roman and 13/19 pt Futura Bold Oblique.

A & C Black uses paper produced with elemental chlorine-free
pulp, harvested from managed sustainable forests.

Printed in China through Colorcraft Ltd., Hong Kong.

I'm Me and You are You

Althea

Photographs by
Charlie Best

Illustrations by
Conny Jude

A & C Black · London

Everyone is different.

I grew up in another country.

I am tall, so people think I'm older than I am.

I wear glasses, some people tease me.

What is different about you? Does it matter to you?

> I wish I had brothers and sisters. There's nobody to play with at home.

There may be things about yourself that you wish you could change.

> I wish I had straight hair, then I could grow it long.

> I want to cut my pigtails. People pull them, but mum says I look better with long hair.

3

You can't judge people by the way they look or the way they speak. You need to talk and get to know them.

Janet said she was bullied at her last school. "When I got a brace on my teeth it made my voice sound funny. I was the same person, but people teased me. It made me feel angry and sad inside."

Adrian says that people underestimate him unfairly. "Just because you are different in one way, it doesn't mean you are different in everything. I'm dyslexic but it doesn't stop me playing football."

Being different can be hard. Lots of people are handicapped in some way. Sometimes in ways we cannot see. People who are dyslexic find it very difficult to learn to read or write because they muddle letters like **b** and **d** and they put letters in the wrong order. People sometimes decide that those who have dyslexia must be dim, but they can be very intelligent.

People can be very cruel to someone just because they are different in some way.

Peter says, "My brother is computer mad. He's not that good at talking. Other people think he's odd, and leave him out. He gets very upset."

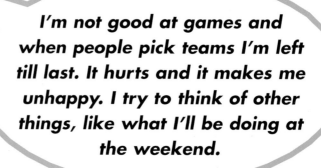

I'm not good at games and when people pick teams I'm left till last. It hurts and it makes me unhappy. I try to think of other things, like what I'll be doing at the weekend.

The people who live next door to us are cheeky and rude and I don't want to play with them. They say I'm stuck up. They make me feel really small even though I'm older than them.

Cathy says, "Sometimes people get at you just because you are different. Then you start feeling different and they get at you even more. They make fun of my clothes which makes me awkward."

No two people see the world in the same way. The way each of us sees the world comes from our past experience, and no two people ever have the same experience, not even identical twins.

"My brother supports Manchester United but I think they're rubbish. I support Arsenal."

Tom said he thought his life was over when he had to wear glasses and have a patch over one eye. "I tried to pretend I didn't need them but I couldn't see the board. I kept getting the answers wrong. When another boy in the school had to wear a patch he pretended he was a pirate. I wish I had been able to make a joke out of it too."

What really matters is not what happens to us, but how we interpret what happens to us. When Tim got 80% for his spelling test he felt bad because he hadn't got a better mark. When Tim's mum said 80% was brilliant because there were some hard words in the test, Tim was happy.

When people don't understand that other people see things differently, they don't bother to find out how others might be thinking and feeling. As a result they can be very hurtful, especially when they tease.

I had problems with my ears. I had to have cotton wool in them. People thought I couldn't hear. They said nasty things in front of me. It made me very unhappy.

It's good if you can stick up for people who are being teased by pointing out how the person who is being teased feels. But it can be difficult to do it all by yourself.

There was a boy in our class, he had glasses and long hair. He was a loner. I felt really sorry for him, but my friends teased him so I went along with them. I feel really bad about it now. I should have had more courage.

Often people don't want to draw attention to themselves as being different.

Umar says that sometimes people tease him because he is very good at maths. "Sometimes I get it wrong on purpose, but they don't notice and I get bad marks."

Chloe says she tries to pretend she's not scared of heights. "People call me chicken."

Izzy is my best friend. We were in a group who said banana sandwiches were yuck, so we said we hated them too. I love banana sandwiches, then I found Izzy does too! We were just afraid to be different.

Sometimes people may decide not to say what they think because they don't want to upset others.

My friend was so pleased with her new sweater. I didn't tell her I didn't like it.

At times it may be best to keep your thoughts to yourself. Other times it's best to say what you think, even though it may take courage to do so.

When I'm on holiday with my cousin I can't play with my cuddly toys. She's older than me and she makes me feel small. I want to impress her.

We usually choose friends who seem to see things in the way we do. But it's a good idea to get to know people who see things quite differently from you because you can then learn a lot and have some interesting experiences. You also learn how to make some good compromises.

I love football but my cousin hates it. He's mad about skating. When I went to stay with him I thought I'd be bored but he took me skating and it was great.

"My friend and I get on most of the time, but she doesn't like playing the same games as me. She gets grumpy and cries. We make it up by laughing."

It would be bland and boring if everyone was the same.

"I was very fed up when Mum said my cousins were coming to stay. Last time they were silly and messed up all my things. Mum said they're bigger now, so they'll probably be more sensible, but I could put away my best toys just in case."

"In fact they were much nicer and we had a really good time together."

Sometimes you may feel you've grown older than your parents give you credit for.

Rory says he feels frustrated when his friends go skating every Saturday afternoon. "My mum won't let me because she says I'm not old enough to go just with my friends and no adult to mind us. I wish she wouldn't treat me like a baby."

Everyone changes as they grow older and gain more experience. We should try to remain open to change all our lives. Change can be scary, but it always means new opportunities. Kate says her sister started at secondary school last year. "She was really scared at first, but now she loves it. They have a big art department and she goes to drama club. I think I'll like it when I get there."

Misunderstandings often arise because we don't understand how other people think or feel.

"Dad was cross all the time, then he said that I couldn't go to France on the school trip. I thought he was getting at me because I'd had a bad school report. I thought he was being mean and I was horrid to him."

"Later Mum told me he was having a difficult time with work and we really couldn't afford the school trip. That made *me* feel really mean."

My older sister is really clever, so the teachers expect me to be too. They get cross when I don't get it right and say I'm messing about. I'm not. I try really hard. I'm just not as brainy as her.

Tom says that when his friend Josh broke his pen he was furious. "I thought he had done it on purpose to get at me. He hadn't, he was very upset. I ended up saying sorry to him."

It's always a good idea to ask people what they think and feel because then we don't jump to wrong conclusions.

19

Sometimes it's difficult for older people to accept differences. Your parents may not agree with your grandparents on the way they think about things. You in turn may not agree with your parents.

Nan looks after me when Mum's at work. She and Mum don't always agree on what I'm allowed to do. When I ask Nan about what it was like when she was young I understand why.

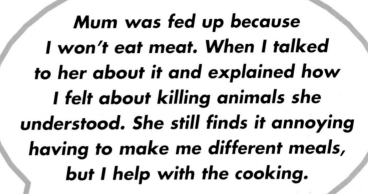

Mum was fed up because I won't eat meat. When I talked to her about it and explained how I felt about killing animals she understood. She still finds it annoying having to make me different meals, but I help with the cooking.

We may have been brought up to hold certain opinions. When we talk to others we find they think differently. School is a place where you can learn to get on with lots of people who may hold very different opinions to yourself.

"We should be free to hold different views, as long as we're not harming others by holding these views. In class we have proper debates. The teacher makes us speak in turn and listen to other people speaking. It's good fun and we go on talking about it afterwards. Sometimes we make new friends that way."

Just because people see things differently from you doesn't mean that they're mad or bad. It's just that they have had different experiences from you.

When other people hold different views from you, it doesn't mean that you can't get along with them and treat their views with respect, even though you don't agree with them.

"If you treat their views with respect then you can demand that they treat your view with respect."

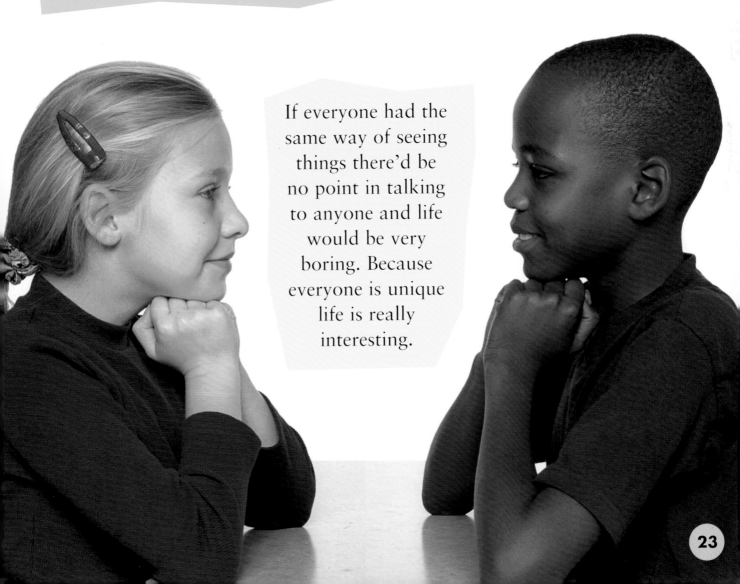

If everyone had the same way of seeing things there'd be no point in talking to anyone and life would be very boring. Because everyone is unique life is really interesting.

For teachers and parents

A note from Dorothy Rowe

What determines a person's behaviour isn't what happens to that person but how that person interprets what has happened. No two people ever interpret anything in exactly the same way because no two people ever have exactly the same experience.

When we don't understand that other people can't help but see things differently from us and we assume that we know how another person thinks and feels, misunderstandings soon arise. We can avoid misunderstandings only by knowing that other people see things differently and having good ways of finding out how other people think and feel.

By believing that anyone who thinks differently from us must be bad or mad, we make possible the very worst in human behaviour, from children bullying other children, through racial and religious violence, to war. Children who feel that their views aren't listened to and respected find it very hard to treat other children with tolerance.

Views differ, but not all views are equally valid or useful. Some views cause problems, some are based solely on fantasy, some are misinformed. Through discussions where different views are compared, children can learn how to look at the consequences of the views they hold, and to check their views against reality.

To start a discussion, ask everyone to give an example of how they think they are different to other people in the class. Discuss whether these differences matter.

The following points may be useful when using the book.

Page 3
Discuss the advantages and disadvantages of being an only child. Many children have step parents, and often have experience of both situations. Learning to live with step brothers and sisters takes time.

Page 4-5
When someone has a mental handicap they may find it difficult to communicate. They may not think as fast or seem to react at all at first. Inside they feel just as deeply as other people.

When someone has a handicap it can be difficult to know how much help to offer them. When someone is different in one aspect it doesn't mean they need help with everything.

Pages 6-7
Some people are cruel without meaning to be. They haven't thought through what it must be like to be the other person. How would you feel if you were always left out? Although people learn to cope, it doesn't mean they are happy inside.

Pages 8-9
We can make our lives easier for ourselves by learning to be positive about ourselves and our abilities.

Pages 10-11
People often think teasing is just a bit of fun. They have no idea of how hurtful they are being. Others may tease or bully because they have been bullied themselves. They do it to make themselves feel important.

Page 12
When a whole group appears to think one way, it takes courage to argue. If you do say how you feel you will often find that others will tell you they agree with you, but didn't have the courage to say so at the time. Many adults feel just as shy in a group.

Page 17
Discuss the parent's point of view. Children have to show parents or other adults that they can behave responsibly. Negotiate a compromise - perhaps a parent could come along and remain in the background?

Moving up to secondary school can be quite scary; it may feel to children as if they've become small fish in a big pond. They have to get used to moving from class to class and being taught by different people for each lesson. Children may worry that they won't be able to find their way around.

Pages 18-19
Children may well be able to come up with other examples of when they have behaved unfairly or been treated unfairly through misunderstandings. Discuss how these misunderstandings could have been avoided.

Page 20
This works both ways as children often disapprove of the way their parents behave (smoking being one big issue).

Page 22
Everyone needs to learn to debate and listen to other people's points of view. We can all learn from each other and broaden our outlook.

Further reading

Children may find it interesting and helpful to have a look at some of the following books which also deal with the subject of individuality and people's responses to difference in others.

Rob Childs
Moving The Goalposts
(A & C Black, 1998)

Mick Gowar
The Gang
(Watts, 1995)

Martina Selway
I Hate Roland Roberts
(Red Fox, 1993)

Lynda Waterhouse
Bonnie Fitch
(Red Fox, 1993)